ON TYRANNY

ON TYRANNY

Twenty Lessons from the Twentieth Century

TIMOTHY SNYDER

TIM
DUGGAN
BOOKS

NEW YORK

Copyright © 2017 by Timothy Snyder

All rights reserved.
Published in the United States by Tim Duggan Books,
an imprint of the Crown Publishing Group, a division of
Penguin Random House LLC, New York.
timdugganbooks.com

TIM DUGGAN BOOKS and the Crown colophon are
trademarks of Penguin Random House LLC.

Library of Congress Cataloging-in-Publication Data is
available upon request.

ISBN 978-0-8041-9011-4
Ebook ISBN 978-0-8041-9012-1

Printed in the United States of America

Book design by Lauren Dong
Cover design by Christopher Brand

30

First Edition

In politics, being deceived is no excuse.

—LESZEK KOŁAKOWSKI

Prologue

History and Tyranny

History does not repeat, but it does instruct. As the Founding Fathers debated our Constitution, they took instruction from the history they knew. Concerned that the democratic republic they envisioned would collapse, they contemplated the descent of ancient democracies and republics into oligarchy and empire. As they knew, Aristotle warned that inequality brought instability, while Plato believed that demagogues exploited free speech to install themselves as tyrants. In founding a democratic republic upon law and establishing a system of checks and balances, the Founding Fathers sought to avoid the evil that they, like the ancient philosophers, called *tyranny*. They had in mind the usurpation of power by a single individual or group, or the circumvention of law by rulers for their own benefit. Much of the succeeding political debate in the United States has concerned the problem of tyranny within American society: over slaves and women, for example.

It is thus a primary American tradition to consider history when our political order seems imperiled. If we worry today that the American experiment is threatened by tyranny, we can follow the example of the Founding Fathers and contemplate the history of other democracies and republics. The good news is that we can draw upon more recent and relevant examples than ancient Greece and Rome. The bad news is that the history of modern democracy is also one of decline and fall. Since the American colonies declared their independence from a British monarchy that the Founders deemed "tyrannical," European history has seen three major democratic moments: after the First World War in 1918, after the Second World War in 1945, and after the end of communism in 1989. Many of the democracies founded at these junctures failed, in circumstances that in some important respects resemble our own.

History can familiarize, and it can warn. In the late nineteenth century, just as in the late twentieth century, the expansion of global trade generated expectations of progress. In the early twentieth century, as in the early twenty-first, these hopes were challenged by new visions of mass politics in which a leader or a party claimed to directly represent the will of the people. European democracies collapsed into right-wing authoritarianism and fascism in the 1920s and '30s. The communist Soviet Union, established in 1922, extended its model into Europe in the 1940s. The European history of the twentieth century shows us that societies can break, democracies can fall, ethics can collapse, and ordinary men can find themselves standing over death pits with guns in their hands. It would serve us well today to understand why.

Both fascism and communism were responses to globalization: to the real and perceived inequalities it created, and the apparent helplessness of the democracies in addressing them. Fascists rejected reason in the name of will, denying objective truth in favor of a glorious myth articulated by leaders who claimed to give voice to the people. They put a face on globalization, arguing that its complex challenges were the result of a conspiracy against the nation. Fascists ruled for a decade or two, leaving behind an intact intellectual legacy that grows more relevant by the day. Communists ruled for longer, for nearly seven decades in the Soviet Union, and more than four decades in much of eastern Europe. They proposed rule by a disciplined party elite with a monopoly on reason that would guide society toward a certain future according to supposedly fixed laws of history.

We might be tempted to think that our democratic heritage automatically protects us from such threats. This is a misguided reflex. In fact, the precedent set by the Founders demands that we examine history to understand the deep sources of tyranny, and to consider the proper responses to it. Americans today are no wiser than the Europeans who saw democracy yield to fascism, Nazism, or communism in the twentieth century. Our one advantage is that we might learn from their experience. Now is a good time to do so.

This book presents twenty lessons from the twentieth century, adapted to the circumstances of today.

ON TYRANNY

1

Do not obey in advance.

Most of the power of authoritarianism is freely given. In times like these, individuals think ahead about what a more repressive government will want, and then offer themselves without being asked. A citizen who adapts in this way is teaching power what it can do.

Anticipatory obedience is a political tragedy. Perhaps rulers did not initially know that citizens were willing to compromise this value or that principle. Perhaps a new regime did not at first have the direct means of influencing citizens one way or another. After the German elections of 1932, which permitted Adolf Hitler to form a government, or the Czechoslovak elections of 1946, where communists were victorious, the next crucial step was anticipatory obedience. Because enough people in both cases voluntarily extended their services to the new leaders, Nazis and communists alike realized that they could move quickly toward a full regime change. The first heedless acts of conformity could not then be reversed.

In early 1938, Adolf Hitler, by then securely in power in Germany, was threatening to annex neighboring Austria. After the Austrian chancellor conceded, it was the Austrians' anticipatory obedience that decided the fate of Austrian Jews. Local Austrian Nazis captured Jews and forced them to scrub the streets to remove symbols of independent Austria. Crucially, people who were not Nazis looked on with interest and amusement. Nazis who had kept lists of Jewish property stole what they could. Crucially, others who were not Nazis joined in the theft. As the political theorist Hannah Arendt remembered, "when German troops invaded the country and Gentile neighbors started riots at Jewish homes, Austrian Jews began to commit suicide."

The anticipatory obedience of Austrians in March 1938 taught the high Nazi leadership what was possible. It was in Vienna that August that Adolf Eichmann established the Central Office for Jewish Emigration. In November 1938, following the Austrian example of March, German Nazis organized the national pogrom known as *Kristallnacht*.

In 1941, when Germany invaded the Soviet Union, the SS took the initiative to devise the methods of mass killing without orders to do so. They guessed what their superiors wanted and demonstrated what was possible. It was far more than Hitler had thought.

At the very beginning, anticipatory obedience means adapting instinctively, without reflecting, to a new situation. Do only Germans do such things? The Yale psychologist Stanley Milgram, contemplating Nazi atrocities, wanted to show that there was a particular authoritarian personality that explained why Germans behaved as they had. He devised an experiment to test the proposition, but failed to get permission to carry it out in Germany. So he undertook it instead in a Yale University building in 1961—at around the same time that Adolf Eichmann was being tried in Jerusalem for his part in the Nazi Holocaust of the Jews.

Milgram told his subjects (some Yale students, some New Haven residents) that they would be applying an electrical shock to other participants in an experiment about learning. In fact, the people attached to the wires on the other side of a window were in on the scheme with Milgram, and only pretended to be shocked. As the subjects (thought they) shocked the (people they thought were) participants in a learning experiment, they saw a horrible sight. People whom they did not know, and against whom they had no grievance, seemed to be suffering greatly—pounding the glass and complaining of heart pain. Even so, most subjects followed Milgram's instructions and continued to apply (what they thought were) ever greater shocks until the victims appeared to die. Even those who did not proceed all the way to the (apparent) killing of their fellow human beings left without inquiring about the health of the other participants.

Milgram grasped that people are remarkably receptive to new rules in a new setting. They are surprisingly willing to harm and kill others in the service of some new purpose if they are so instructed by a new authority. "I found so much obedience," Milgram remembered, "that I hardly saw the need for taking the experiment to Germany."

2

Defend institutions.

It is institutions that help us to preserve decency. They need our help as well. Do not speak of "our institutions" unless you make them yours by acting on their behalf. Institutions do not protect themselves. They fall one after the other unless each is defended from the beginning. So choose an institution you care about—a court, a newspaper, a law, a labor union—and take its side.

We tend to assume that institutions will automatically maintain themselves against even the most direct attacks. This was the very mistake that some German Jews made about Hitler and the Nazis after they had formed a government. On February 2, 1933, for example, a leading newspaper for German Jews published an editorial expressing this mislaid trust:

> We do not subscribe to the view that Mr. Hitler and his friends, now finally in possession of the power they have so long desired, will implement the proposals circulating in [Nazi newspapers]; they will not suddenly deprive German Jews of their constitutional rights, nor enclose them in ghettos, nor subject them to the jealous and murderous impulses of the mob. They cannot do this because a number of crucial factors hold powers in check . . . and they clearly do not want to go down that road. When one acts as a European power, the whole atmosphere tends towards ethical

reflection upon one's better self and away from revisiting one's earlier oppositional posture.

Such was the view of many reasonable people in 1933, just as it is the view of many reasonable people now. The mistake is to assume that rulers who came to power through institutions cannot change or destroy those very institutions—even when that is exactly what they have announced that they will do. Revolutionaries sometimes do intend to destroy institutions all at once. This was the approach of the Russian Bolsheviks. Sometimes institutions are deprived of vitality and function, turned into a simulacrum of what they once were, so that they gird the new order rather than resisting it. This is what the Nazis called *Gleichschaltung.*

It took less than a year for the new Nazi order to consolidate. By the end of 1933, Germany had become a one-party state in which all major institutions had been humbled. That November, German authorities held parliamentary elections (without opposition) and a referendum (on an issue where the "correct" answer was known) to confirm the new order. Some German Jews voted as the Nazi leaders wanted them to in the hope that this gesture of loyalty would bind the new system to them. That was a vain hope.

3

Beware the one-party state.

The parties that remade states and suppressed rivals were not omnipotent from the start. They exploited a historic moment to make political life impossible for their opponents. So support the multi-party system and defend the rules of democratic elections. Vote in local and state elections while you can. Consider running for office.

Thomas Jefferson probably never said that "eternal vigilance is the price of liberty," but other Americans of his era certainly did. When we think of this saying today, we imagine our own righteous vigilance directed outward, against misguided and hostile others. We see ourselves as a city on the hill, a stronghold of democracy, looking out for threats that come from abroad. But the sense of the saying was entirely different: that human nature is such that American democracy must be defended from *Americans* who would exploit its freedoms to bring about its end. The American abolitionist Wendell Phillips did in fact say that "eternal vigilance is the price of liberty." He added that "the manna of popular liberty must be gathered each day or it is rotten."

The record of modern European democracy confirmed the wisdom of those words. The twentieth century saw earnest attempts to extend the franchise and establish durable democracies. Yet the democracies that arose after the First World War (and the Second) often collapsed when a single party seized power in some combination of an election and a coup d'état. A party emboldened by a favorable election result or motivated by ideology, or both, might change the system from within. When fascists or Nazis or communists did well in elections in the 1930s or '40s, what followed was some combination of spectacle, repression, and salami tactics—slicing off layers of opposition one by one. Most people were distracted, some were imprisoned, and others were outmatched.

The hero of a David Lodge novel says that you don't know, when you make love for the last time, that you are making love for the last time. Voting is like that. Some of the Germans who voted for the Nazi Party in 1932 no doubt understood that this might be the last meaningfully free election for some time, but most did not. Some of the Czechs and Slovaks who voted for the Czechoslovak Communist Party in 1946 probably realized that they were voting for the end of democracy, but most assumed they would have another chance. No doubt the Russians who voted in 1990 did not think that this would be the last free and fair election in their country's history, which (thus far) it has been. Any election can be the last, or at least the last in the lifetime of the person casting the vote. The Nazis remained in power until they lost a world war in 1945, the Czechoslovak communists until their system collapsed in 1989. The Russian oligarchy established after the 1990 elections continues to function, and promotes a foreign policy designed to destroy democracy elsewhere.

Does the history of tyranny apply to the United States? Certainly the early Americans who spoke of "eternal vigilance" would have thought so. The logic of the system they devised was to mitigate the consequences of our real imperfections, not to celebrate our imaginary perfection. We certainly face, as did the ancient Greeks, the problem of oligarchy—ever more threatening as globalization increases differences in wealth. The odd American idea that giving money to political campaigns is free speech means that the very rich have far more speech, and so in effect far more voting power, than other citizens. We believe that we have checks and balances, but have rarely faced a situation like the present: when the less popular of the two parties controls every lever of power at the federal level, as well as the majority of statehouses. The party that exercises such control proposes few policies that are popular with the society at large, and several that are generally unpopular—and thus must either fear democracy or weaken it.

Another early American proverb held that "where annual elections end, tyranny begins." Will we come to see one of our own elections much as Russians see the elections of 1990, or Czechs the elections of 1946, or Germans the elections of 1932? This, for now, depends upon us. Much needs to be done to fix the gerrymandered system so that each citizen has one equal vote, and so that each vote can be simply counted by a fellow citizen. We need paper ballots, because they cannot be tampered with remotely and can always be recounted. This sort of work can be done at the local and state levels. Any future elections will be a test of American traditions.

4

Take responsibility for the face of the world.

The symbols of today enable the reality of tomorrow. Notice the swastikas and the other signs of hate. Do not look away, and do not get used to them. Remove them yourself and set an example for others to do so.

Life is political, not because the world cares about how you feel, but because the world reacts to what you do. The minor choices we make are themselves a kind of vote, making it more or less likely that free and fair elections will be held in the future. In the politics of the everyday, our words and gestures, or their absence, count very much. A few extreme (and less extreme) examples from the twentieth century can show us how.

In the Soviet Union under the rule of Joseph Stalin, prosperous farmers were portrayed on propaganda posters as pigs—a dehumanization that in a rural setting clearly suggests slaughter. This was in the early 1930s, as the Soviet state tried to master the countryside and extract capital for crash industrialization. The peasants who had more land or livestock than others were the first to lose what they had. A neighbor portrayed as a pig is someone whose land you can take. But those who followed the symbolic logic became victims in their turn. Having turned the poorer peasants against the richer, Soviet power then seized everyone's land for the new collective farms. Collectivization, when completed, brought starvation to much of the Soviet peasantry. Millions of people in Soviet Ukraine, Soviet Kazakhstan, and Soviet Russia died horrible and humiliating deaths between 1930 and 1933. Before it was over, Soviet citizens were butchering corpses for human meat.

In 1933, as the starvation in the USSR reached its height, the Nazi Party came to power in Germany. In the euphoria of victory, Nazis tried to organize a boycott of Jewish shops. This was not very successful at first. But the practice of marking one firm as "Jewish" and another as "Aryan" with paint on the windows or walls did affect the way Germans thought about household economics. A shop marked "Jewish" had no future. It became an object of covetous plans. As property was marked as ethnic, envy transformed ethics. If shops could be "Jewish," what about other companies and properties? The wish that Jews might disappear, perhaps suppressed at first, rose as it was leavened by greed. Thus the Germans who marked shops as "Jewish" participated in the process by which Jews really did disappear—as did people who simply looked on. Accepting the markings as a natural part of the urban landscape was already a compromise with a murderous future.

You might one day be offered the opportunity to display symbols of loyalty. Make sure that such symbols include your fellow citizens rather than exclude them. Even the history of lapel pins is far from innocent. In Nazi Germany in 1933, people wore lapel pins that said "Yes" during the elections and referendum that confirmed the one-party state. In Austria in 1938, people who had not previously been Nazis began to wear swastika pins. What might seem like a gesture of pride can be a source of exclusion. In the Europe of the 1930s and '40s, some people chose to wear swastikas, and then others had to wear yellow stars.

The late history of communism, when no one believed in the revolution anymore, offers a final lesson about symbols. Even when citizens are demoralized and wish only to be left alone, public markers can still sustain a tyrannical regime. When Czechoslovak communists won elections in 1946 and then proceeded to claim full power after a coup in 1948, many Czechoslovak citizens were euphoric. When the dissident thinker Václav Havel wrote "The Power of the Powerless" three decades later, in 1978, he was explaining the continuity of an oppressive regime in whose goals and ideology few people still believed. He offered a parable of a greengrocer who places a sign reading "Workers of the world, unite!" in his shop window.

It is not that the man actually endorses the content of this quotation from *The Communist Manifesto*. He places the sign in his window so that he can withdraw into daily life without trouble from the authorities. When everyone else follows the same logic, the public sphere is covered with signs of loyalty, and resistance becomes unthinkable. As Havel put it:

We have seen that the real meaning of the green-grocer's slogan has nothing to do with what the text of the slogan actually says. Even so, the real meaning is quite clear and generally comprehensible because the code is so familiar: the greengrocer declares his loyalty in the only way the regime is capable of hearing; that is, by accepting the prescribed ritual, by accepting appearances as reality, by accepting the given rules of the game, thus making it possible for the game to go on, for it to exist in the first place.

And what happens, asked Havel, if no one plays the game?

5

Remember professional ethics.

When political leaders set a negative example, professional commitments to just practice become more important. It is hard to subvert a rule-of-law state without lawyers, or to hold show trials without judges. Authoritarians need obedient civil servants, and concentration camp directors seek businessmen interested in cheap labor.

Before the Second World War, a man named Hans Frank was Hitler's personal lawyer. After Germany invaded Poland in 1939, Frank became the governor-general of occupied Poland, a German colony where millions of Jews and other Polish citizens were murdered. He once boasted that there were not enough trees to make the paper for posters that would be needed to announce all of the executions. Frank claimed that law was meant to serve the race, and so what seemed good for the race was therefore the law. With arguments like this, German lawyers could convince themselves that laws and rules were there to serve their projects of conquest and destruction, rather than to hinder them.

The man Hitler chose to oversee the annexation of Austria, Arthur Seyss-Inquart, was a lawyer who later ran the occupation of the Netherlands. Lawyers were vastly overrepresented among the commanders of the *Einsatzgruppen*, the special task forces who carried out the mass murder of Jews, Gypsies, Polish elites, communists, the handicapped, and others. German (and other) physicians took part in ghastly medical experiments in the concentration camps. Businessmen from I.G. Farben and other German firms exploited the labor of concentration camp inmates, Jews in ghettos, and prisoners of war. Civil servants, from ministers down to secretaries, oversaw and recorded it all.

If lawyers had followed the norm of no execution without trial, if doctors had accepted the rule of no surgery without consent, if businessmen had endorsed the prohibition of slavery, if bureaucrats had refused to handle paperwork involving murder, then the Nazi regime would have been much harder pressed to carry out the atrocities by which we remember it.

Professions can create forms of ethical conversation that are impossible between a lonely individual and a distant government. If members of professions think of themselves as groups with common interests, with norms and rules that oblige them at all times, then they can gain confidence and indeed a certain kind of power. Professional ethics must guide us precisely when we are told that the situation is exceptional. Then there is no such thing as "just following orders." If members of the professions confuse their specific ethics with the emotions of the moment, however, they can find themselves saying and doing things that they might previously have thought unimaginable.

6

Be wary of paramilitaries.

When the men with guns who have always claimed to be against the system start wearing uniforms and marching with torches and pictures of a leader, the end is nigh. When the pro-leader paramilitary and the official police and military intermingle, the end has come.

Most governments, most of the time, seek to monopolize violence. If only the government can legitimately use force, and this use is constrained by law, then the forms of politics that we take for granted become possible. It is impossible to carry out democratic elections, try cases at court, design and enforce laws, or indeed manage any of the other quiet business of government when agencies beyond the state also have access to violence. For just this reason, people and parties who wish to undermine democracy and the rule of law create and fund violent organizations that involve themselves in politics. Such groups can take the form of a paramilitary wing of a political party, the personal bodyguard of a particular politician—or apparently spontaneous citizens' initiatives, which usually turn out to have been organized by a party or its leader.

Armed groups first degrade a political order, and then transform it. Violent right-wing groups, such as the Iron Guard in interwar Romania or the Arrow Cross in interwar Hungary, intimidated their rivals. Nazi storm troopers began as a security detail clearing the halls of Hitler's opponents during his rallies. As paramilitaries known as the SA and the SS, they created a climate of fear that helped the Nazi Party in the parliamentary elections of 1932 and 1933. In Austria in 1938 it was the local SA that quickly took advantage of the absence of the usual local authority to loot, beat, and humiliate Jews, thereby changing the rules of politics and preparing the way for the Nazi takeover of the country. It was the SS that ran the German concentration camps—lawless zones where ordinary rules did not apply. During the Second World War, the SS extended the lawlessness it had pioneered in the camps to whole European countries under German occupation. The SS began as an organization outside the law, became an organization that transcended the law, and ended up as an organization that undid the law.

Because the American federal government

uses mercenaries in warfare and American state governments pay corporations to run prisons and internment camps, the use of violence in the United States is already highly privatized. What was novel in 2016 was a candidate who ordered a private security detail to clear opponents from rallies and encouraged the audience itself to remove people who expressed different opinions. A protestor would first be greeted with boos, then with frenetic cries of "USA," and then be forced to leave the rally. At one campaign rally the candidate said, "There's a remnant left over. Maybe get the remnant out. Get the remnant out." The crowd, taking its cue, then tried to root out other people who might be dissenters, all the while crying "USA." The candidate interjected: "Isn't this more fun than a regular boring rally? To me, it's fun." This kind of mob violence was meant to transform the political atmosphere, and it did.

For violence to transform not just the atmosphere but also the system, the emotions of rallies and the ideology of exclusion have to be incorporated into the training of armed guards. These first challenge the police and military, then penetrate the police and military, and finally transform the police and military.

7

Be reflective if you must be armed.

If you carry a weapon in public service, may God bless you and keep you. But know that evils of the past involved policemen and soldiers finding themselves, one day, doing irregular things. Be ready to say no.

Authoritarian regimes usually include a special riot police force whose task is to disperse citizens who seek to protest, and a secret state police force whose assignments include the murder of dissenters or others designated as enemies. And indeed we find forces of the latter kind deeply involved in the great atrocities of the twentieth century, such as the Great Terror in the Soviet Union of 1937–38 and the Holocaust of European Jews perpetrated by Nazi Germany in 1941–45. Yet we make a great mistake if we imagine that the Soviet NKVD or the Nazi SS acted without support. Without the assistance of regular police forces, and sometimes regular soldiers, they could not have killed on such a large scale.

In the Great Terror in the Soviet Union, NKVD officers recorded 682,691 executions of supposed enemies of the state, most of them peasants or members of national minorities. Perhaps no organ of violence has ever been more centralized or better organized than the NKVD of those years. A small number of men carried out the neck shots, which meant that certain NKVD officers had thousands of political murders on their consciences. Even so, they could not possibly have carried out this campaign without the assistance of local police forces, legal professionals, and civil servants throughout the Soviet Union. The Great Terror took place during a state of exception that required all policemen to subordinate themselves to the NKVD and its special tasks. The policemen were not the principal perpetrators, but they provided the indispensable manpower.

When we think of the Nazi Holocaust of the Jews, we imagine Auschwitz and mechanized impersonal death. This was a convenient way for Germans to remember the Holocaust, since they could claim that few of them had known exactly what had happened behind those gates. In fact, the Holocaust began not in the death facilities, but over shooting pits in eastern Europe. And indeed some of the commanders of the *Einsatzgruppen*, the German task forces that perpetrated some of the murders, were tried at Nuremberg and later in

West German courts. But even these trials were a kind of minimization of the scale of the crime. Not the SS commanders alone, but essentially all of the thousands of men who served under their command were murderers.

And this was just the beginning. Every large-scale shooting action of the Holocaust (more than thirty-three thousand Jews murdered outside Kyiv, more than twenty-eight thousand outside Riga, and on and on) involved the regular German police. All in all, regular policemen murdered more Jews than the *Einsatzgruppen*. Many of them had no special preparation for this task. They found themselves in an unknown land, they had their orders, and they did not want to look weak. In the rare cases when they refused these orders to murder Jews, policemen were not punished.

Some killed from murderous conviction. But many others who killed were just afraid to stand out. Other forces were at work besides conformism. But without the conformists, the great atrocities would have been impossible.

8

Stand out.

Someone has to. It is easy to follow along. It can feel strange to do or say something different. But without that unease, there is no freedom. Remember Rosa Parks. The moment you set an example, the spell of the status quo is broken, and others will follow.

After the Second World War, Europeans, Americans, and others created myths of righteous resistance to Hitler. In the 1930s, however, the dominant attitudes had been accommodation and admiration. By 1940 most Europeans had made their peace with the seemingly irresistible power of Nazi Germany. Influential Americans such as Charles Lindbergh opposed war with the Nazis under the slogan "America First." It is those who were considered exceptional, eccentric, or even insane in their own time—those who did not change when the world around them did—whom we remember and admire today.

Well before the Second World War, numerous European states had abandoned democracy for some form of right-wing authoritarianism. Italy became the first fascist state in 1922, and was a military ally of Germany. Hungary, Romania, and Bulgaria had been drawn toward Germany by the promise of trade and territory. In March 1938 none of the great powers offered any resistance as Germany annexed Austria. In September 1938 the great powers—France, Italy, and Great Britain, then led by Neville Chamberlain—actually cooperated with Nazi Germany in the partition of Czechoslovakia. In summer 1939 the Soviet Union allied with Nazi Germany and the Red Army joined the *Wehrmacht* in the invasion of Poland. The Polish government chose to fight, activating agreements that brought Great Britain and France into the war. Germany, supplied with food and fuel by the Soviet Union, invaded and quickly occupied Norway, the Netherlands, Belgium, and even France in the spring of 1940. The remainder of the British expeditionary force was evacuated from the Continent at Dunkirk in late May and early June 1940.

When Winston Churchill became prime minister in May 1940, Great Britain was alone. The British had won no meaningful battles and had no important allies. They had entered the war to support Poland, a cause that seemed lost. Nazi Germany and its Soviet ally dominated the continent. The Soviet Union had invaded Finland in November 1939, beginning with a bombing of Helsinki. Right after Churchill assumed office, the Soviet Union occupied and annexed the three Baltic states of Estonia, Latvia, and Lithuania. The United States had not entered the war.

Adolf Hitler had no special animus toward Britain or its empire, and indeed imagined a division of the world into spheres of interests. He expected Churchill to come to terms after the fall of France. Churchill did not. He told the French that "whatever you may do, we shall fight on for ever and ever and ever."

In June 1940, Churchill told the British parliament that "the battle of Britain is about to begin." The German *Luftwaffe* began the bombing of British cities. Hitler expected that this would force Churchill to sign an armistice, but he was mistaken. Churchill later called the air campaign "a time when it was equally good to live or die." He spoke of "the buoyant and imperturbable temper of Britain which I had the honor to express." In fact he himself helped the British to define themselves as a proud people who would calmly resist evil. Other politicians would have found support in British public opinion to end the war. Churchill instead resisted, inspired, and won. The Royal Air Force (including two Polish squadrons and a number of other foreign pilots) held back the *Luftwaffe*. Without control of the air, even Hitler could not imagine an amphibious invasion of Great Britain.

Churchill did what others had not done. Rather than concede in advance, he forced Hitler to change his plans. The essential German strategy had been to remove any resistance in the west, and then to invade (thus betraying) the Soviet Union and colonize its western territories. In June 1941, with Britain still in the war, Germany attacked its Soviet ally.

Now Berlin had to fight a two-front war, and Moscow and London were suddenly unexpected allies. In December 1941, Japan bombed the American naval base at Pearl Harbor in Hawaii, and the United States entered the war.

Now Moscow, Washington, and London formed a grand and irresistible coalition. Together, and with the help of many other allies, these three great powers won the Second World War. But had Churchill not kept Britain in the war in 1940, there would have been no such war to fight.

Churchill said that history would be kind to him, because he intended to write it himself. Yet in his vast histories and memoirs, he presented his own decisions as self-evident, and credited the British people and Britain's allies. Today what Churchill did seems normal, and right. But at the time he had to stand out.

Of course, Great Britain was only in the war because the Polish leadership had chosen to fight in September 1939. Open Polish armed resistance was overcome that October. In 1940, the character of the German occupation was becoming clear in the Polish capital, Warsaw.

Teresa Prekerowa was meant to finish high school that year. Her family lost its property to the Germans and was forced to move to Warsaw and rent. Her father was arrested. One of her uncles was killed in battle. Two of her brothers were in German prisoner-of-war camps. Warsaw itself had been heavily damaged by a German air campaign, which had killed about twenty-five thousand people.

Teresa, a very young woman, stood out among her friends and family in her reaction to this horror. At a time when it was natural to think only of oneself, she thought of others. In late 1940, the Germans began to establish ghettos in the part of Poland under their control. That October, the Jews of Warsaw and the surrounding region were required to move to a certain district of the city. One of Teresa's brothers had been friendly with a Jewish girl and her family before the war. Teresa now observed that people quietly allowed their Jewish friends to slip away from their lives.

Without telling her family, and at great risk to herself, Teresa chose to enter the Warsaw ghetto a dozen times in late 1940, bringing food and medicine to Jews she knew and Jews she did not. By the end of the year she had persuaded her brother's friend to escape the ghetto. In 1942 Teresa helped the girl's parents and brother to escape. That summer in the Warsaw ghetto, the Germans carried out what they called the "Great Action," deporting some 265,040 Jews to the death factory at Treblinka to be murdered and killing another 10,380 Jews in the ghetto itself. Teresa saved a family from certain death.

Teresa Prekerowa later became a historian of the Holocaust, writing about the Warsaw ghetto and about others who helped to aid Jews. But she preferred not to write about herself. When, much later, she was asked to speak about her own life, she called her actions normal. From our perspective, her actions seem exceptional. She stood out.

9

Be kind to our language.

Avoid pronouncing the phrases everyone else does. Think up your own way of speaking, even if only to convey that thing you think everyone is saying. Make an effort to separate yourself from the internet. Read books.

Victor Klemperer, a literary scholar of Jewish origin, turned his philological training against Nazi propaganda. He noticed how Hitler's language rejected legitimate opposition: *The people* always meant some people and not others (the president uses the word in this way), encounters were always *struggles* (the president says *winning*), and any attempt by free people to understand the world in a different way was *defamation* of the leader (or, as the president puts it, *libel*).

Politicians in our times feed their clichés to television, where even those who wish to disagree repeat them. Television purports to challenge political language by conveying images, but the succession from one frame to another can hinder a sense of resolution. Everything happens fast, but nothing actually happens. Each story on televised news is "breaking" until it is displaced by the next one. So we are hit by wave upon wave but never see the ocean.

The effort to define the shape and significance of events requires words and concepts that elude us when we are entranced by visual stimuli. Watching televised news is sometimes little more than looking at someone who is also looking at a picture. We take this collective trance to be normal. We have slowly fallen into it.

More than half a century ago, the classic novels of totalitarianism warned of the domination of screens, the suppression of books, the narrowing of vocabularies, and the associated difficulties of thought. In Ray Bradbury's *Fahrenheit 451*, published in 1953, firemen find and burn books while most citizens watch interactive television. In George Orwell's *1984*, published in 1949, books are banned and television is two-way, allowing the government to observe citizens at all times. In *1984*, the language of visual media is highly constrained, to starve the public of the concepts needed to think about the present, remember the past, and consider the future. One of the regime's projects is to limit the language further by eliminating ever more words with each edition of the official dictionary.

Staring at screens is perhaps unavoidable, but the two-dimensional world makes little sense unless we can draw upon a mental armory that we have developed somewhere else. When we repeat the same words and phrases that appear in the daily media, we accept the absence of a larger framework. To have such a framework requires more concepts, and having more concepts requires reading. So get the screens out of your room and surround yourself with books. The characters in Orwell's and Bradbury's books could not do this—but we still can.

What to read? Any good novel enlivens our ability to think about ambiguous situations and judge the intentions of others. Fyodor Dostoevsky's *The Brothers Karamazov* and Milan Kundera's *The Unbearable Lightness of Being* might suit our moment. Sinclair Lewis's novel *It Can't Happen Here* is perhaps not a great work of art; Philip Roth's *The Plot Against America* is better. One novel known by millions of young Americans that offers an account of tyranny and resistance is

J. K. Rowling's *Harry Potter and the Deathly Hallows*. If you or your friends or your children did not read it that way the first time, then it bears reading again.

Some of the political and historical texts that inform the arguments made here are "Politics and the English Language" by George Orwell (1946); *The Language of the Third Reich* by Victor Klemperer (1947); *The Origins of Totalitarianism* by Hannah Arendt (1951); *The Rebel* by Albert Camus (1951); *The Captive Mind* by Czesław Miłosz (1953); "The Power of the Powerless" by Václav Havel (1978); "How to Be a Conservative-Liberal-Socialist" by Leszek Kołakowski (1978); *The Uses of Adversity* by Timothy Garton Ash (1989); *The Burden of Responsibility* by Tony Judt (1998); *Ordinary Men* by Christopher Browning (1992); and *Nothing Is True and Everything Is Possible* by Peter Pomerantsev (2014).

Christians might return to the foundational book, which as ever is very timely. Jesus preached that it "is easier for a camel to go through the eye of a needle than for a rich man to enter into the kingdom of God." We should be modest, for "whosoever shall exalt himself shall be abased; and he that shall humble himself shall be exalted." And of course we must be concerned with what is true and what is false: "And ye shall know the truth, and the truth shall make you free."

10

Believe in truth.

To abandon facts is to abandon freedom. If nothing is true, then no one can criticize power, because there is no basis upon which to do so. If nothing is true, then all is spectacle. The biggest wallet pays for the most blinding lights.

You submit to tyranny when you renounce the difference between what you want to hear and what is actually the case. This renunciation of reality can feel natural and pleasant, but the result is your demise as an individual—and thus the collapse of any political system that depends upon individualism. As observers of totalitarianism such as Victor Klemperer noticed, truth dies in four modes.

The first mode is the open hostility to verifiable reality, which takes the form of presenting inventions and lies as if they were facts. The president does this at a high rate and at a fast pace. One attempt during the 2016 campaign to track his utterances found that 78 percent of his factual claims were false. This proportion is so high that it makes the correct assertions seem like unintended oversights on the path toward total fiction. Demeaning the world as it is begins the creation of a fictional counterworld.

The second mode is shamanistic incantation. As Klemperer noted, the fascist style depends upon "endless repetition," designed to make the fictional plausible and the criminal desirable. The systematic use of nicknames such as "Lyin' Ted" and "Crooked Hillary" displaced certain character traits that might more appropriately have been affixed to the president himself. Yet through blunt repetition over Twitter, our president managed the transformation of individuals into stereotypes that people then spoke aloud. At rallies, the repeated chants of "Build that wall" and "Lock her up" did not describe anything that the president had specific plans to do, but their very grandiosity established a connection between him and his audience.

The next mode is magical thinking, or the open embrace of contradiction. The president's campaign involved the promises of cutting taxes for everyone, eliminating the national debt, and increasing spending on both social policy and national defense. These promises mutually contradict. It is as if a farmer said he were taking an egg from the henhouse, boiling it whole and serving it to his wife, and also poaching it and serving it to his children, and then returning it to the hen unbroken, and then watching as the chick hatches.

Accepting untruth of this radical kind requires a blatant abandonment of reason. Klemperer's descriptions of losing friends in Germany in 1933 over the issue of magical thinking ring eerily true today. One of his former students implored him to "abandon yourself to your feelings, and you must always focus on the *Führer*'s greatness, rather than on the discomfort you are feeling at present." Twelve years later, after all the atrocities, and at the end of a war that Germany had clearly lost, an amputated soldier told Klemperer that Hitler "has never lied yet. I believe in Hitler."

The final mode is misplaced faith. It involves the sort of self-deifying claims the president made when he said that "I alone can solve it" or "I am your voice." When faith descends from heaven to earth in this way, no room remains for the small truths of our individual discernment and experience. What terrified Klemperer was the way that this transition seemed permanent. Once truth had become oracular rather than factual, evidence was irrelevant. At the end of the war a worker told Klemperer that "understanding is useless, you have to have faith. I believe in the *Führer*."

Eugène Ionesco, the great Romanian playwright, watched one friend after another slip away into the language of fascism in the 1930s. The experience became the basis for his 1959 absurdist play, *Rhinoceros*, in which those who fall prey to propaganda are transformed into giant horned beasts. Of his own personal experiences Ionesco wrote:

> *University professors, students, intellectuals were turning Nazi, becoming Iron Guards, one after the other. At the beginning, certainly they were not Nazis. About fifteen of us would get together to talk and to try to find arguments opposing theirs. It was not easy. . . . From time to time, one of our friends said: "I don't agree with them, to be sure, but on certain points, nevertheless,*

I must admit, for example, the Jews . . . ," etc. And this was a symptom. Three weeks later, this person would become a Nazi. He was caught in the mechanism, he accepted everything, he became a rhinoceros. Towards the end, only three or four of us were still resisting.

Ionesco's aim was to help us see just how bizarre propaganda actually is, but how normal it seems to those who yield to it. By using the absurd image of the rhinoceros, Ionesco was trying to shock people into noticing the strangeness of what was actually happening.

The rhinoceri are roaming through our neurological savannahs. We now find ourselves very much concerned with something we call "post-truth," and we tend to think that its scorn of everyday facts and its construction of alternative realities is something new or postmodern. Yet there is little here that George Orwell did not capture seven decades ago in his notion of "doublethink." In its philosophy, post-truth restores precisely the fascist attitude to truth—and that is why nothing in our own world would startle Klemperer or Ionesco.

Fascists despised the small truths of daily existence, loved slogans that resonated like a new religion, and preferred creative myths to history or journalism. They used new media, which at the time was radio, to create a drumbeat of propaganda that aroused feelings before people had time to ascertain facts. And now, as then, many people confused faith in a hugely flawed leader with the truth about the world we all share.

Post-truth is pre-fascism.

11

Investigate.

Figure things out for yourself. Spend more time with long articles. Subsidize investigative journalism by subscribing to print media. Realize that some of what is on the internet is there to harm you. Learn about sites that investigate propaganda campaigns (some of which come from abroad). Take responsibility for what you communicate with others.

What is truth?" Sometimes people ask this question because they wish to do nothing. Generic cynicism makes us feel hip and alternative even as we slip along with our fellow citizens into a morass of indifference. It is your ability to discern facts that makes you an individual, and our collective trust in common knowledge that makes us a society. The individual who investigates is also the citizen who builds. The leader who dislikes the investigators is a potential tyrant.

During his campaign, the president claimed on a Russian propaganda outlet that American "media has been unbelievably dishonest." He banned many reporters from his rallies, and regularly elicited hatred of journalists from the public. Like the leaders of authoritarian regimes, he promised to suppress freedom of speech by laws that would prevent criticism. Like Hitler, the president used the word *lies* to mean statements of fact not to his liking, and presented journalism as a campaign against himself. Where the Nazis said "Lügenpresse," he said "Fake news." The president was on friendlier terms with the internet, his source for erroneous information that he passed on to millions of people.

In 1971, contemplating the lies told in the United States about the Vietnam War, the political theorist Hannah Arendt took comfort in the inherent power of facts to overcome falsehoods in a free society: "Under normal circumstances the liar is defeated by reality, for which there is no substitute; no matter how large the tissue of falsehood that an experienced liar has to offer, it will never be large enough, even if he enlists the help of computers, to cover the immensity of factuality." The part about computers is no longer true. In the 2016 presidential election, the two-dimensional world of the internet was more important than the three-dimensional world of human contact. People going door-to-door to canvass encountered the surprised blinking of American citizens who realized that they would have to talk about politics with a flesh-and-blood human being rather than having their views affirmed by their Facebook feeds. Within the two-dimensional internet world, new collectivities have arisen, invisible by the light of day—tribes with distinct worldviews, beholden to manipulations. (And yes, there is a conspiracy that you can find online: It is the one to keep you online, looking for conspiracies.)

We need print journalists so that stories can develop on the page and in our minds. What does it mean, for example, that the president says that women belong "at home," that pregnancy is an "inconvenience," that mothers do not give "100 percent" at work, that women should be punished for having abortions, that women are "slobs," "pigs," or "dogs," and that it is permissible to sexually assault them? What does it mean that six of the president's companies have gone bankrupt, and that the president's enterprises have been financed by mysterious infusions of cash from entities in Russia and Kazakhstan? We can learn these things on various media. When we learn them from a screen, however, we tend to be drawn in by the logic of spectacle. When we learn of one scandal, it whets our appetite for the next.

Once we subliminally accept that we are watching a reality show rather than thinking about real life, no image can actually hurt the president politically. Reality television must become more dramatic with each episode. If we found a video of the president performing Cossack dances while Vladimir Putin claps, we would probably just demand the same thing with the president wearing a bear suit and holding rubles in his mouth.

The better print journalists allow us to consider the meaning, for ourselves and our country, of what might otherwise seem to be isolated bits of information. But while anyone can repost an article, researching and writing is hard work that requires time and money. Before you deride the "mainstream media," note that it is no longer the mainstream. It is derision that is mainstream and easy, and actual journalism that is edgy and difficult. So try for yourself to write a proper article, involving work in the real world: traveling, interviewing, maintaining relationships with sources, researching in written records, verifying everything, writing and revising drafts, all on a tight and unforgiving schedule. If you find you like doing this, keep a blog. In the meantime, give credit to those who do all of that for a living. Journalists are not perfect, any more than people in other vocations are perfect. But the work of people who adhere to journalistic ethics is of a different quality than the work of those who do not.

We find it natural that we pay for a plumber or a mechanic, but demand our news for free. If we did not pay for plumbing or auto repair, we would not expect to drink water or drive cars. Why then should we form our political judgment on the basis of zero investment? We get what we pay for.

If we do pursue the facts, the internet gives us enviable power to convey them. The authorities cited here had nothing of the kind. Leszek Kołakowski, the great Polish philosopher and historian from whom this book takes its epigraph, lost his chair at Warsaw University for speaking out against the communist regime, and could not publish. The first quotation in this book, from Hannah Arendt, came from a pamphlet entitled "We Refugees," a miraculous achievement written by someone who had escaped a murderous Nazi regime. A brilliant mind like Victor Klemperer, much admired today, is remembered only because he stubbornly kept a hidden diary under Nazi rule. For him it was sustenance: "My diary was my balancing pole, without which I would have fallen down a thousand times." Václav Havel, the most important thinker among the communist dissidents of the 1970s, dedicated his most important essay, "The Power of the Powerless," to a philosopher who died shortly after interrogation by the Czechoslovak communist secret police. In communist Czechoslovakia, this pamphlet had to be circulated illegally, in a few copies, as what east Europeans at the time, following the Russian dissidents, called "samizdat."

"If the main pillar of the system is living a lie," wrote Havel, "then it is not surprising that the fundamental threat to it is living in truth."

Since in the age of the internet we are all publishers, each of us bears some private responsibility for the public's sense of truth. If we are serious about seeking the facts, we can each make a small revolution in the way the internet works. If you are verifying information for yourself, you will not send on fake news to others. If you choose to follow reporters whom you have reason to trust, you can also transmit what they have learned to others. If you retweet only the work of humans who have followed journalistic protocols, you are less likely to debase your brain interacting with bots and trolls.

We do not see the minds that we hurt when we publish falsehoods, but that does not mean we do no harm. Think of driving a car. We may not see the other driver, but we know not to run into their car. We know that the damage will be mutual. We protect the other person without seeing him, dozens of times every day. Likewise, although we may not see the other person in front of his or her computer, we have our share of responsibility for what is on the screen. If we can avoid doing violence to the minds of unseen others on the internet, others will learn to do the same. And then perhaps our internet traffic will cease to look like one great, bloody accident.

12
Make eye contact and small talk.

This is not just polite. It is part of being a citizen and a responsible member of society. It is also a way to stay in touch with your surroundings, break down social barriers, and understand whom you should and should not trust. If we enter a culture of denunciation, you will want to know the psychological landscape of your daily life.

Tyrannical regimes arose at different times and places in the Europe of the twentieth century, but memoirs of their victims all share a single tender moment. Whether the recollection is of fascist Italy in the 1920s, of Nazi Germany of the 1930s, of the Soviet Union during the Great Terror of 1937–38, or of the purges in communist eastern Europe in the 1940s and '50s, people who were living in fear of repression remembered how their neighbors treated them. A smile, a handshake, or a word of greeting—banal gestures in a normal situation—took on great significance. When friends, colleagues, and acquaintances looked away or crossed the street to avoid contact, fear grew. You might not be sure, today or tomorrow, who feels threatened in the United States. But if you affirm everyone, you can be sure that certain people will feel better.

In the most dangerous of times, those who escape and survive generally know people whom they can trust. Having old friends is the politics of last resort. And making new ones is the first step toward change.

13

Practice corporeal politics.

Power wants your body softening in your chair
and your emotions dissipating on the screen.
Get outside. Put your body in unfamiliar places
with unfamiliar people. Make new friends and
march with them.

For resistance to succeed, two boundaries must be crossed. First, ideas about change must engage people of various backgrounds who do not agree about everything. Second, people must find themselves in places that are not their homes, and among groups who were not previously their friends. Protest can be organized through social media, but nothing is real that does not end on the streets. If tyrants feel no consequences for their actions in the three-dimensional world, nothing will change.

The one example of successful resistance to communism was the Solidarity labor movement in Poland in 1980–81: a coalition of workers and professionals, elements of the Roman Catholic Church, and secular groups. Its leaders had learned hard lessons under communism. In 1968, the regime mobilized workers against students who protested. In 1970, when a strike in Gdańsk on the Baltic coast was bloodily suppressed, it was the workers' turn to feel isolated. In 1976, however, intellectuals and professionals formed a group to assist workers who had been abused by the government. These were people from both the Right and the Left, believers and atheists, who created trust among workers—people whom they would not otherwise have met.

When Polish workers on the Baltic coast went on strike again in 1980, they were joined by lawyers, scholars, and others who helped them make their case. The result was the creation of a free labor union, as well as government guarantees to observe human rights. During the sixteen months that Solidarity was legal, ten million people joined, and countless new friendships were created amid strikes, marches, and demonstrations. The Polish communist regime put down the movement with martial law in 1981. Yet eight years later, in 1989, when they needed negotiating partners, the communists had to turn to Solidarity. The labor union insisted on elections, which it then won. This was the beginning of the end of communism in Poland, eastern Europe, and the Soviet Union.

The choice to be in public depends on the ability to maintain a private sphere of life. We are free only when it is we ourselves who draw the line between when we are seen and when we are not seen.

14

Establish a private life.

Nastier rulers will use what they know about you to push you around. Scrub your computer of malware on a regular basis. Remember that email is skywriting. Consider using alternative forms of the internet, or simply using it less. Have personal exchanges in person. For the same reason, resolve any legal trouble. Tyrants seek the hook on which to hang you. Try not to have hooks.

What the great political thinker Hannah Arendt meant by *totalitarianism* was not an all-powerful state, but the erasure of the difference between private and public life. We are free only insofar as we exercise control over what people know about us, and in what circumstances they come to know it. During the campaign of 2016, Americans took a step toward totalitarianism without even noticing by accepting as normal the violation of electronic privacy. Whether it is done by American or Russian intelligence agencies, or for that matter by any institution, the theft, discussion, or publication of personal communications destroys a basic foundation of our rights. If we have no control over who reads what and when, we have no ability to act in the present or plan for the future. Whoever can pierce your privacy can humiliate you and disrupt your relationships at will. No one (except perhaps a tyrant) has a private life that can survive public exposure by hostile directive.

The timed email bombs of the 2016 presidential campaign were also a powerful form of disinformation. Words written in one situation make sense only in that context. The very act of removing them from their historical moment and dropping them in another is an act of falsification. What is worse, when media followed the email bombs as if they were news, they betrayed their own mission. Few journalists made an effort to explain why people said or wrote the things they did at the time. Meanwhile, in transmitting the privacy violations as news, the media allowed themselves to be distracted from the actual events of the day. Rather than reporting the violation of basic rights, our media generally preferred to mindlessly indulge the inherently salacious interest we have in other people's affairs.

Our appetite for the secret, thought Arendt, is dangerously political. Totalitarianism removes the difference between private and public not just to make individuals unfree, but also to draw the whole society away from normal politics and toward conspiracy theories. Rather than defining facts or generating interpretations, we are seduced by the notion of hidden realities and dark conspiracies that explain everything. As we learned from these email bombs, this mechanism works even when what is revealed is of no interest. The revelation of what was once confidential becomes the story itself. (It is striking that news media are much worse at this than, say, fashion or sports reporters. Fashion reporters know that models are taking off their clothes in the changing rooms, and sports reporters know that athletes shower in the locker room, but neither allow private matters to supplant the public story they are supposed to be covering.)

When we take an active interest in matters of doubtful relevance at moments that are chosen by tyrants, oligarchs and spooks, we participate in the demolition of our own political order. To be sure, we might feel that we are doing nothing more than going along with everyone else. This is true—and it is what Arendt described as the devolution of a society into a "mob." We can try to solve this problem individually, by securing our own computers; we can also try to solve it collectively, by supporting, for example, organizations that are concerned with human rights.

15

Contribute to good causes.

Be active in organizations, political or not, that express your own view of life. Pick a charity or two and set up autopay. Then you will have made a free choice that supports civil society and helps others to do good.

It is gratifying to know that, whatever the course of events, you are helping others to do good. Many of us can afford to support some part of the vast network of charities that one of our former presidents called "a thousand points of light." Those points of light are best seen, like stars at dusk, against a darkening sky.

When Americans think of freedom, we usually imagine a contest between a lone individual and a powerful government. We tend to conclude that the individual should be empowered and the government kept at bay. This is all well and good. But one element of freedom is the choice of associates, and one defense of freedom is the activity of groups to sustain their members. This is why we should engage in activities that are of interest to us, our friends, our families. These need not be expressly political: Václav Havel, the Czech dissident thinker, gave the example of brewing good beer.

Insofar as we take pride in these activities, and come to know others who do so as well, we are creating civil society. Sharing in an undertaking teaches us that we can trust people beyond a narrow circle of friends and families, and helps us to recognize authorities from whom we can learn. The capacity for trust and learning can make life seem less chaotic and mysterious, and democratic politics more plausible and attractive.

The anticommunist dissidents of eastern Europe, facing a situation more extreme than ours, recognized the seemingly nonpolitical activity of civil society as an expression and a safeguard of freedom. They were right. In the twentieth century, all the major enemies of freedom were hostile to non-governmental organizations, charities, and the like. Communists required all such groups to be officially registered and transformed them into institutions of control. Fascists created what they called a "corporatist" system, in which every human activity had its proper place, subordinated to the party-state. Today's authoritarians (in India, Turkey, Russia, China) are also highly allergic to the idea of free associations and non-governmental organizations.

16

Learn from peers in other countries.

Keep up your friendships abroad, or make new friends in other countries. The present difficulties in the United States are an element of a larger trend. And no country is going to find a solution by itself. Make sure you and your family have passports.

In the year before the president was elected, American journalists were often mistaken about his campaign. As he surmounted barrier after barrier and accumulated victory after victory, our commentariat assured us that at the next stage he would be stopped by one fine American institution or another. There was, meanwhile, one group of observers who took a different position: east Europeans and those who study eastern Europe. To them, much about the president's campaign was familiar, and the final outcome was no surprise. Ukrainian and Russian journalists who sniffed the air in the Midwest said more realistic things than American pollsters who had built careers on understanding the politics of their own country.

To Ukrainians, Americans seemed comically slow to react to the obvious threats of cyberwar and targeted lies. When Russian propaganda made Ukraine a target in 2013, young Ukrainian journalists and others reacted immediately, decisively, and sometimes humorously with campaigns to expose disinformation. Russia deployed many of the same techniques against Ukraine that it later used against the United States—while invading Ukraine. When Russian media falsely claimed in 2014 that Ukrainian troops crucified a small boy, the Ukrainian response was rapid and effective (at least within Ukraine itself). When Russian media spread the story in 2016 that Hillary Clinton was ill because she mentioned an article on "decision fatigue" (which is not an illness) in an email, the story was spread by Americans. The Ukrainians won, and the Americans lost, in the sense that Russia failed to get the regime it wanted in its neighbor, but did see its preferred candidate triumph in the United States. This should give us pause. History, which for a time seemed to be running from west to east, now seems to be moving from east to west. Everything that happens here seems to happen there first.

The fact that most Americans do not have passports has become a problem for American democracy. Sometimes Americans say that they do not need travel documents, because they prefer to die defending freedom in America. These are fine words, but they miss an important point. The fight will be a long one. Even if it does require sacrifice, it first demands sustained attention to the world around us, so that we know what we are resisting, and how best to do so. So having a passport is not a sign of surrender. On the contrary, it is liberating, since it creates the possibility of new experiences. It allows us to see how other people, sometimes wiser than we, react to similar problems. Since so much of what is happening now is familiar to the rest of the world or from recent history, we must observe and listen.

17
Listen for dangerous words.

Be alert to the use of the words *extremism* and *terrorism*. Be alive to the fatal notions of *emergency* and *exception*. Be angry about the treacherous use of patriotic vocabulary.

The most intelligent of the Nazis, the legal theorist Carl Schmitt, explained in clear language the essence of fascist governance. The way to destroy all rules, he explained, was to focus on the idea of the *exception*. A Nazi leader outmaneuvers his opponents by manufacturing a general conviction that the present moment is exceptional, and then transforming that state of exception into a permanent emergency. Citizens then trade real freedom for fake safety.

When politicians today invoke *terrorism* they are speaking, of course, of an actual danger. But when they try to train us to surrender freedom in the name of safety, we should be on our guard. There is no necessary tradeoff between the two. Sometimes we do indeed gain one by losing the other, and sometimes not. People who assure you that you can *only* gain security at the price of liberty usually want to deny you both.

You can certainly concede freedom without becoming more secure. The feeling of submission to authority might be comforting, but it is not the same thing as actual safety. Likewise, gaining a bit of freedom may be unnerving, but this momentary unease is not dangerous. It is easy to imagine situations where we sacrifice both freedom and safety at the same time: when we enter an abusive relationship or vote for a fascist. Similarly, it is none too difficult to imagine choices that increase both freedom and safety, like leaving an abusive relationship or emigrating from a fascist state. It is the government's job to increase both freedom and security.

Extremism certainly sounds bad, and governments often try to make it sound worse by using the word *terrorism* in the same sentence. But the word has little meaning. There is no doctrine called *extremism*. When tyrants speak of *extremists*, they just mean people who are not in the mainstream—as the tyrants themselves are defining that mainstream at that particular moment. Dissidents of the twentieth century, whether they were resisting fascism or communism, were called *extremists*. Modern authoritarian regimes, such as Russia, use laws on *extremism* to punish those who criticize their policies. In this way the notion of *extremism* comes to mean virtually everything except what is, in fact, extreme: tyranny.

18

Be calm when the unthinkable arrives.

Modern tyranny is terror management. When the terrorist attack comes, remember that authoritarians exploit such events in order to consolidate power. The sudden disaster that requires the end of checks and balances, the dissolution of opposition parties, the suspension of freedom of expression, the right to a fair trial, and so on, is the oldest trick in the Hitlerian book. *Do not fall for it.*

The Reichstag fire was the moment when Hitler's government, which came to power mainly through democratic means, became the menacingly permanent Nazi regime. It is the archetype of terror management.

On February 27, 1933, at about nine p.m., the building housing the German parliament, the Reichstag, began to burn. Who set the fire that night in Berlin? We don't know, and it doesn't really matter. What matters is that this spectacular act of terror initiated the politics of emergency. Gazing with pleasure at the flames that night, Hitler said: "This fire is just the beginning." Whether or not the Nazis set the fire, Hitler saw the political opportunity: "There will be no mercy now. Anyone standing in our way will be cut down." The next day a decree suspended the basic rights of all German citizens, allowing them to be "preventively detained" by the police. On the strength of Hitler's claim that the fire was the work of Germany's enemies, the Nazi Party won a decisive victory in parliamentary elections on

March 5. The police and the Nazi paramilitaries began to round up members of left-wing political parties and place them in improvised concentration camps. On March 23 the new parliament passed an "enabling act," which allowed Hitler to rule by decree. Germany then remained in a state of emergency for the next twelve years, until the end of the Second World War. Hitler had used an act of terror, an event of limited inherent significance, to institute a regime of terror that killed millions of people and changed the world.

The authoritarians of today are also terror managers, and if anything they are rather more creative. Consider the current Russian regime, so admired by the president. Vladimir Putin not only came to power in an incident that strikingly resembled the Reichstag fire, he then used a series of terror attacks—real, questionable, and fake—to remove obstacles to total power in Russia and to assault democratic neighbors.

When Putin was appointed prime minister by a failing Boris Yeltsin in August 1999, he was an unknown with a nugatory approval rating. The following month a series of buildings were bombed in Russian cities, apparently by the Russian secret state police. Its officers were arrested by their own colleagues with evidence of their guilt; in another case the speaker of the Russian parliament announced an explosion a few days *before* it took place. Nonetheless, Putin declared a war of revenge against Russia's Muslim population in Chechnya, promising to pursue the supposed perpetrators and "rub them out in the shithouse."

The Russian nation rallied; Putin's approval ratings skyrocketed; the following March he won presidential elections. In 2002, after Russian security forces killed scores of Russian civilians while suppressing a real terrorist attack at a Moscow theater, Putin exploited the occasion to seize control of private television. After a school in Beslan was besieged by terrorists in 2004 (in strange circumstances that suggested a provocation), Putin did away with the position of elected regional governors. Thus Putin's rise to power and his elimination of two major institutions—private television and elected regional governorships—were enabled by the management of real, fake, and questionable terrorism.

After Putin returned to the presidency in 2012, Russia introduced terror management into its foreign policy. In its invasion of Ukraine in 2014, Russia transformed units of its own regular army into a terrorist force, removing insignia from uniforms and denying all responsibility for the dreadful suffering they inflicted. In the campaign for the Donbas region of southeastern Ukraine, Russia deployed Chechen irregulars and sent units of its regular army based in Muslim regions to join the invasion. Russia also tried (but failed) to hack the 2014 Ukrainian presidential election.

In April 2015, Russian hackers took over the transmission of a French television station, pretended to be ISIS, and then broadcast material designed to terrorize France. Russia impersonated a "cybercaliphate" so that the French would fear terror more than they already did. The aim was presumably to drive voters to the Far-Right National Front, a party financially supported by Russia. After 130 people were killed and 368 injured in the terrorist attack on Paris of November 2015, the founder of a think tank close to the Kremlin rejoiced that terrorism would drive Europe toward fascism and Russia. Both fake and real Islamic terrorism in western Europe, in other words, were thought to be in the Russian interest.

In early 2016, Russia manufactured a moment of fake terror in Germany. While bombing Syrian civilians and thus driving Muslim refugees to Europe, Russia exploited a family drama to instruct Germans that Muslims were rapists of children. The aim, again, seems to have been to destabilize a democratic system and promote the parties of the extreme right.

The previous September, the German government had announced that it would take half a million refugees from the war in Syria. Russia then began a bombing campaign in Syria that targeted civilians. Having provided the refugees, Russia then supplied the narrative. In January 2016, the Russian mass media spread a story that a girl of Russian origin in Germany who had momentarily gone missing had been serially raped by Muslim immigrants. With suspicious alacrity, right-wing organizations in Germany organized protests against the government. When the local police informed the population that no such rape had taken place, Russian media accused them of a cover-up. Even Russian diplomats joined the spectacle.

When the American president speaks of fighting terrorism alongside Russia, what he is proposing to the American people is terror management: the exploitation of real, dubious, and simulated terror attacks to bring down democracy. The Russian recap of the first telephone call between the president and Vladimir Putin is telling: The two men "shared the opinion that it is necessary to join forces against the common enemy number one: international terrorism and extremism."

For tyrants, the lesson of the Reichstag fire is that one moment of shock enables an eternity of submission. For us, the lesson is that our natural fear and grief must not enable the destruction of our institutions. Courage does not mean not fearing, or not grieving. It does mean recognizing and resisting terror management right away, from the moment of the attack, precisely when it seems most difficult to do so.

James Madison nicely made the point that tyranny arises "on some favorable emergency." After the Reichstag fire, Hannah Arendt wrote that "I was no longer of the opinion that one can simply be a bystander."

19

Be a patriot.

Set a good example of what America means for the generations to come. They will need it.

What is patriotism? Let us begin with what patriotism is not. It is not patriotic to dodge the draft and to mock war heroes and their families. It is not patriotic to discriminate against active-duty members of the armed forces in one's companies, or to campaign to keep disabled veterans away from one's property. It is not patriotic to compare one's search for sexual partners in New York with the military service in Vietnam that one has dodged. It is not patriotic to avoid paying taxes, especially when American working families do pay. It is not patriotic to ask those working, taxpaying American families to finance one's own presidential campaign, and then to spend their contributions in one's own companies.

It is not patriotic to admire foreign dictators. It is not patriotic to cultivate a relationship with Muammar Gaddafi; or to say that Bashar al-Assad and Vladimir Putin are superior leaders. It is not patriotic to call upon Russia to intervene in an American presidential election. It is not patriotic to cite Russian propaganda at rallies.

It is not patriotic to share an adviser with Russian oligarchs. It is not patriotic to solicit foreign policy advice from someone who owns shares in a Russian energy company. It is not patriotic to read a foreign policy speech written by someone on the payroll of a Russian energy company. It is not patriotic to appoint a national security adviser who has taken money from a Russian propaganda organ. It is not patriotic to appoint as secretary of state an oilman with Russian financial interests who is the director of a Russian-American energy company and has received the "Order of Friendship" from Putin.

The point is not that Russia and America must be enemies. The point is that patriotism involves serving *your own country*.

The president is a nationalist, which is not at all the same thing as a patriot. A nationalist encourages us to be our worst, and then tells us that we are the best. A nationalist, "although endlessly brooding on power, victory, defeat, revenge," wrote Orwell, tends to be "uninterested in what happens in the real world." Nationalism is relativist, since the only truth is the resentment we feel when we contemplate others. As the novelist Danilo Kiš put it, nationalism "has no universal values, aesthetic or ethical."

A patriot, by contrast, wants the nation to live up to its ideals, which means asking us to be our best selves. A patriot must be concerned with the real world, which is the only place where his country can be loved and sustained. A patriot has universal values, standards by which he judges his nation, always wishing it well—and wishing that it would do better.

Democracy failed in Europe in the 1920s, '30s, and '40s, and it is failing not only in much of Europe but in many parts of the world today. It is that history and experience that reveals to us the dark range of our possible futures. A nationalist will say that "it can't happen here," which is the first step toward disaster. A patriot says that it could happen here, but that we will stop it.

20
Be as courageous as you can.

If none of us is prepared to die for freedom, then all of us will die under tyranny.

Epilogue

History and Liberty

In Shakespeare's drama *Hamlet,* the hero is a virtuous man who is rightly shocked by the abrupt rise of an evil ruler. Haunted by visions, overcome by nightmares, lonely and estranged, he feels that he must reconstruct his sense of time. "The time is out of joint," says Hamlet. "O cursed spite,/ That ever I was born to set it right!" Our time is certainly out of joint. We have forgotten history for one reason and, if we are not careful, we will neglect it for another. We will have to repair our own sense of time if we wish to renew our commitment to liberty.

Until recently, we Americans had convinced ourselves that there was nothing in the future but more of the same. The seemingly distant traumas of fascism, Nazism, and communism seemed to be receding into irrelevance. We allowed ourselves to accept the *politics of inevitability,* the sense that history could move in only one direction: toward liberal democracy. After communism in eastern Europe came to an end in 1989–91, we imbibed the myth of an "end of history." In doing so, we lowered our defenses, constrained our imagination, and opened the way for precisely the kinds of regimes we told ourselves could never return.

To be sure, the politics of inevitability seem at first glance to be a kind of history. Inevitability politicians do not deny that there is a past, a present, and a future. They even allow for the colorful variety of the distant past. Yet they portray the present simply as a step toward a future that we already know, one of expanding globalization, deepening reason, and growing prosperity. This is what is called a teleology: a narration of time that leads toward a certain, usually desirable, goal. Communism also offered a teleology, promising an inevitable socialist utopia. When that story was shattered a quarter century ago, we drew the wrong conclusion: Rather than rejecting teleologies, we imagined that our own story was true.

The politics of inevitability is a self-induced intellectual coma. So long as there was a contest between communist and capitalist systems, and so long as the memory of fascism and Nazism was alive, Americans had to pay some attention to history and preserve the concepts that allowed them to imagine alternative futures. Yet once we accepted the politics of inevitability, we assumed that history was no longer relevant. If everything in the past is governed by a known tendency, then there is no need to learn the details.

The acceptance of inevitability stilted the way we talked about politics in the twenty-first century. It stifled policy debate and tended to generate party systems where one political party defended the status quo, while the other proposed total negation. We learned to say that there was "no alternative" to the basic order of things, a sensibility that the Lithuanian political theorist Leonidas Donskis called "liquid evil." Once inevitability was taken for granted, criticism indeed became slippery. What appeared to be critical analysis often assumed that the status quo could not actually change, and thereby indirectly reinforced it.

Some spoke critically of *neoliberalism*, the sense that the idea of the free market has somehow crowded out all others. This was true enough, but the very use of the word was usually a kowtow before an unchangeable hegemony. Other critics spoke of the need for *disruption*, borrowing a term from the analysis of technological innovations. When applied to politics, it again carries the implication that nothing can really change, that the chaos that excites us will eventually be absorbed by a self-regulating system. The man who runs naked across a football field certainly disrupts, but he does not change the rules of the game. The whole notion of disruption is adolescent: It assumes that after the teenagers make a mess, the adults will come and clean it up.

But there are no adults. We own this mess.

The second antihistorical way of considering the past is the *politics of eternity*. Like the politics of inevitability, the politics of eternity performs a masquerade of history, though a different one. It is concerned with the past, but in a self-absorbed way, free of any real concern with facts. Its mood is a longing for past moments that never really happened during epochs that were, in fact, disastrous. Eternity politicians bring us the past as a vast misty courtyard of illegible monuments to national victimhood, all of them equally distant from the present, all of them equally accessible for manipulation. Every reference to the past seems to involve an attack by some external enemy upon the purity of the nation.

National populists are eternity politicians. Their preferred reference point is the era when democratic republics seemed vanquished and their Nazi and Soviet rivals unstoppable: the 1930s. Those who advocated Brexit, the departure of the United Kingdom from the European Union, imagined a British nation-state, though such a thing never existed. There was a British Empire, and then there was Britain as a member of the European Union. The move to separate from the EU is not a step backward onto firm ground, but a leap into the unknown. Eerily, when judges said that a parliamentary vote was required for Brexit, a British tabloid called them "enemies of the people"—a Stalinist term from the show trials of the 1930s. The National Front in France urges voters to reject Europe in the name of an imaginary prewar French nation-state. But France, like Britain, has never existed without either an empire or a European project. Leaders of Russia, Poland, and Hungary alike make similar gestures toward a glowing image of the 1930s.

In his 2016 campaign, the American president used the slogan "America First," which is the name of a committee that sought to prevent the United States from opposing Nazi Germany. The president's strategic adviser promised policies that would be "as exciting as the 1930s." When exactly was the "again" in the president's slogan "Make America great again"? Hint: It is the same "again" that we find in "Never again." The president himself has described a regime change in the style of the 1930s as the solution to the problems of the present: "You know what solves it? When the economy crashes, when the country goes to total hell and everything is a disaster." What we need, he thinks, are "riots to go back to where we used to be when we were great."

In the politics of eternity, the seduction by a mythicized past prevents us from thinking about possible futures. The habit of dwelling on victimhood dulls the impulse of self-correction. Since the nation is defined by its inherent virtue rather than by its future potential, politics becomes a discussion of good and evil rather than a discussion of possible solutions to real problems. Since the crisis is permanent, the sense of emergency is always present; planning for the future seems impossible or even disloyal. How can we even think of reform when the enemy is always at the gate?

If the politics of inevitability is like a coma, the politics of eternity is like hypnosis: We stare at the spinning vortex of cyclical myth until we fall into a trance—and then we do something shocking at someone else's orders.

The danger we now face is of a passage from the politics of inevitability to the politics of eternity, from a naive and flawed sort of democratic republic to a confused and cynical sort of fascist oligarchy. The politics of inevitability is terribly vulnerable to the kind of shock it has just received. When something shatters the myth, when our time falls out of joint, we scramble to find some other way to organize what we experience. The path of least resistance leads directly from inevitability to eternity. If you once believed that everything always turns out well in the end, you can be persuaded that nothing turns out well in the end. If you once did nothing because you thought progress is inevitable, then you can continue to do nothing because you think time moves in repeating cycles.

Both of these positions, inevitability and eternity, are antihistorical. The only thing that stands between them is history itself. History allows us to see patterns and make judgments. It sketches for us the structures within which we can seek freedom. It reveals moments, each one of them different, none entirely unique. To understand one moment is to see the possibility of being the cocreator of another. History permits us to be responsible: not for everything, but for something. The Polish poet Czesław Miłosz thought that such a notion of responsibility worked against loneliness and indifference. History gives us the company of those who have done and suffered more than we have.

By embracing the politics of inevitability, we

raised a generation without history. How will these young Americans react now that the promise of inevitability has been so obviously broken? Perhaps they will slide from inevitability toward eternity. It must be hoped that they could, instead, become a historical generation, rejecting the traps of inevitability and eternity that older generations have laid before them. One thing is certain: If young people do not begin to make history, politicians of eternity and inevitability will destroy it. And to make history, young Americans will have to know some. This is not the end, but a beginning.

"The time is out of joint. O cursed spite,/That ever I was born to set it right!" Thus Hamlet. Yet he concludes: "Nay, come, let's go together."

About the Author

TIMOTHY SNYDER is the Levin Professor of History at Yale University. He is the author of *Bloodlands: Europe Between Hitler and Stalin* and *Black Earth: The Holocaust as History and Warning*. Snyder is a member of the Committee on Conscience of the United States Holocaust Memorial Museum and a permanent fellow of the Institute for Human Sciences in Vienna.